KISS

FOR EASY GUITAR

Cover photo by Fin Costello/Redferns/RETNA LTD.

ISBN 978-0-7935-4276-5

HAL•LEONARD® CORPORATION

7777 W. BLUEMOUND RD. P.O. BOX 13819 MILWAUKEE, WI 53213

Visit Hal Leonard Online at
www.halleonard.com

KISS

FOR EASY GUITAR

STRUM AND PICK PATTERNS

This chart contains the suggested strum and pick patterns that are referred to by number at the beginning
of each song in this book. The symbols ⊓ and ∨ in the strum patterns refer to down and up strokes, respectively.
The letters in the pick patterns indicate which right-hand fingers plays which strings.

p = thumb
i = index finger
m = middle finger
a = ring finger

For example; Pick Pattern 2
is played: thumb - index - middle - ring

Strum Patterns   ## Pick Patterns

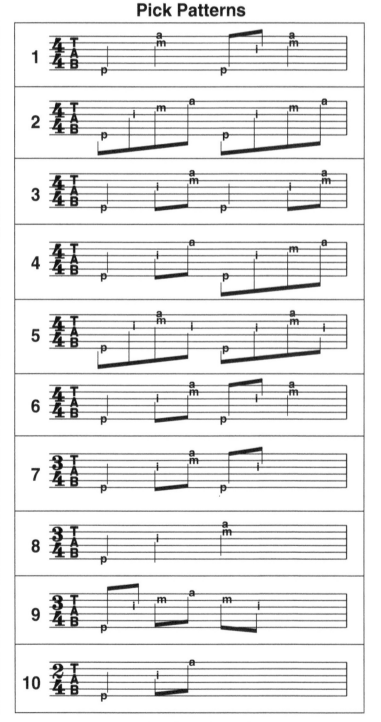

You can use the 3/4 Strum or Pick Patterns in songs written in compound meter (6/8, 9/8, 12/8, etc.).
For example, you can accompany a song in 6/8 by playing the 3/4 pattern twice in each measure.
The 4/4 Strum and Pick Patterns can be used for songs written in cut time (¢) by doubling the note
time values in the patterns. Each pattern would therefore last two measures in cut time.

Calling Dr. Love

Words and Music by Gene Simmons

𝄋 Chorus

Christine Sixteen

Words and Music by Gene Simmons

Strum Pattern: 2, 6
Pick Pattern: 4, 6

Intro
Moderate Rock

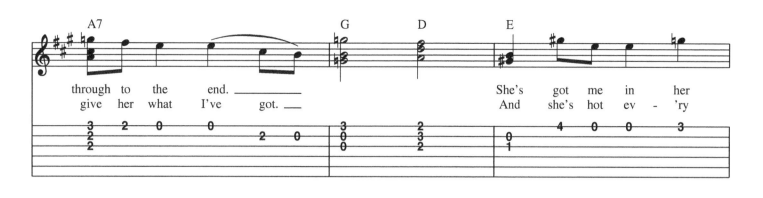

through to the end. _____ She's got me in her
give her what I've got. _____ And she's hot ev - 'ry

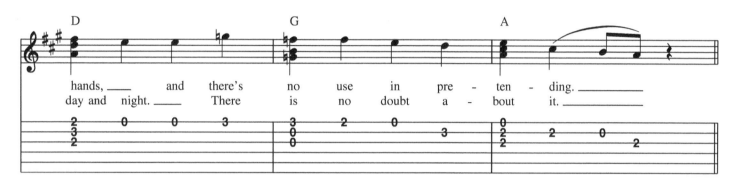

hands, _____ and there's no use in pre - ten - ding. _____
day and night. _____ There is no doubt a - bout it. _____

%𝄋 **Chorus**

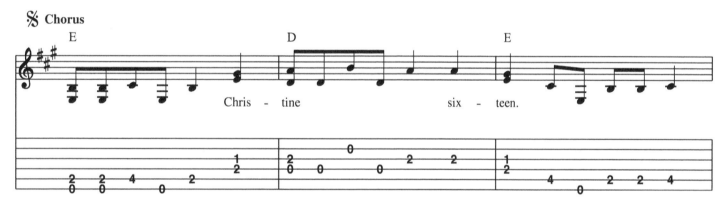

Chris - tine six - teen.

Chris - tine six -

To Coda ⊕

Bridge

teen.   She's been a - round,   but she's young and

Detroit Rock City

Words and Music by Paul Stanley and Bob Ezrin

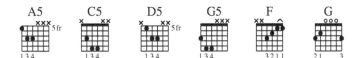

Strum Pattern: 1
Pick Pattern: 1

Intro

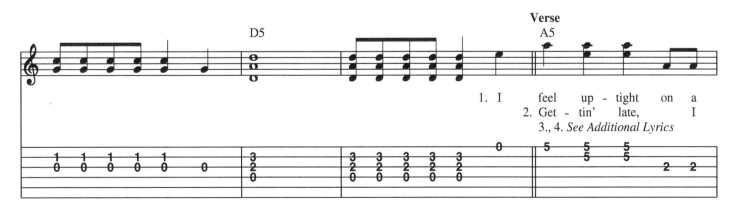

1. I feel up - tight on a
2. Get - tin' late, I
3., 4. *See Additional Lyrics*

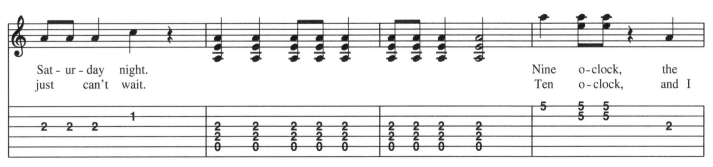

Sat - ur - day night.
just can't wait.

Nine o-clock, the
Ten o-clock, and I

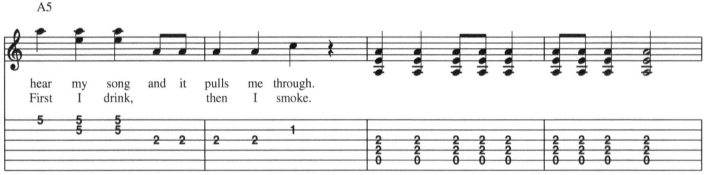

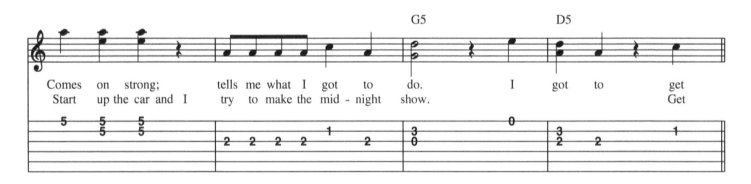

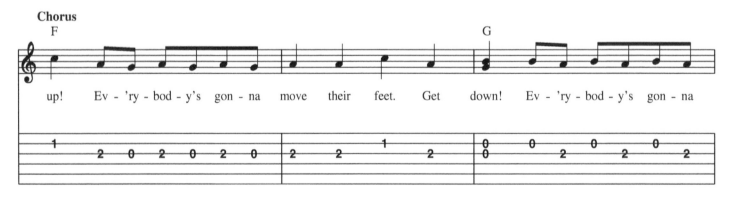

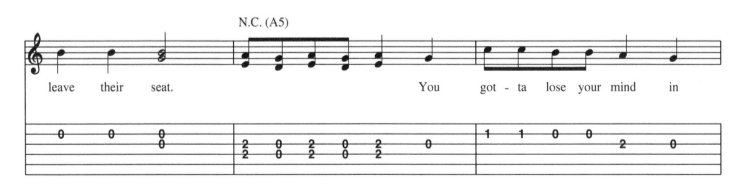

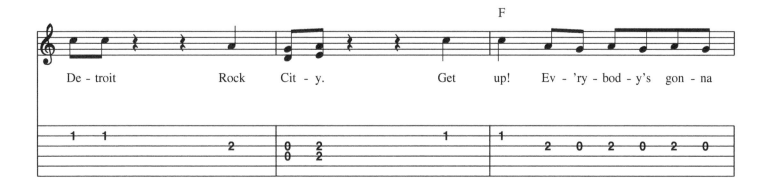

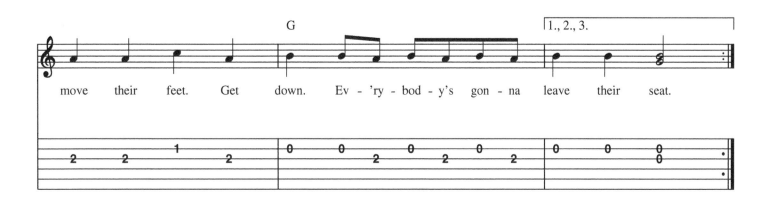

Additional Lyrics

3. Movin' fast doin' ninety five.
   Hit top speed, but I'm still movin' much too slow.
   Feel so good; I'm so alive.
   Hear my song, playin' on the radio. It goes;

4. Twelve o'clock, I gotta rock.
   There's a truck ahead, lights starin' at my eyes.
   Whoa, my God, no time to turn,
   I got to laugh, 'cause I know I'm gonna die. Why?

Cold Gin

Words and Music by Ace Frehley

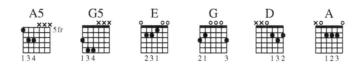

A5   G5   E   G   D   A

Intro

Moderate Rock

N.C.(A)

Strum Pattern: 5
Pick Pattern: 5

Verse

1. Heat - er's ___ broke and I'm a so ___ tired.
time to ___ leave and get an - oth - er ___ quart

I need some ___ fuel to build a fi - re. ___
a - round the cor - ner at the liq - uor store. ___

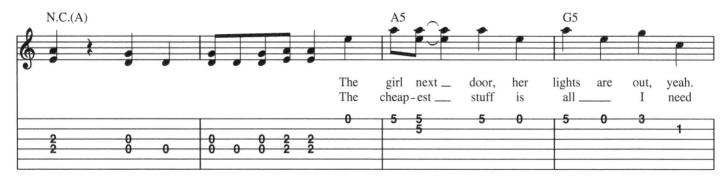

The girl next ___ door, her lights are out, yeah.
The cheap - est ___ stuff is all ___ I need

Deuce

Words and Music by Gene Simmons

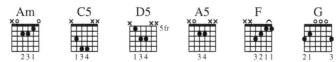

Strum Pattern: 2, 3
Pick Pattern: 2, 3

Intro
Moderate Rock

N.C.

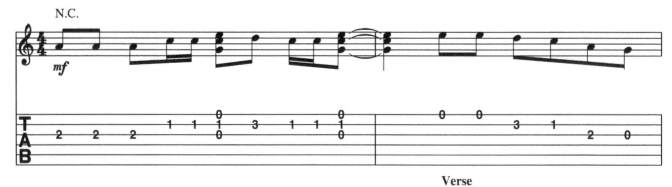

Verse
Am

1. Get up   and get your
2. Hon - ey,   don't push your

C5   D5   N.C.

grand - ma   out   of here.
man   be - hind   his years.

And

Am   C5   D5   N.C.

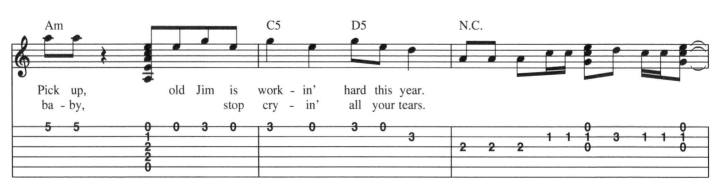

Pick up,   old Jim is work - in'   hard this year.
ba - by,   stop cry - in'   all your tears.

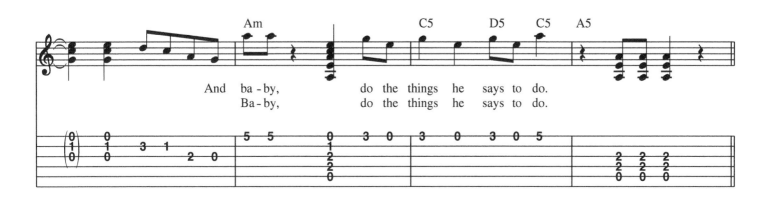

And ba - by, do the things he says to do.
Ba - by, do the things he says to do.

Chorus

Ba - by, if you're feel - in' good, and ba - by, if you're feel - in' nice,

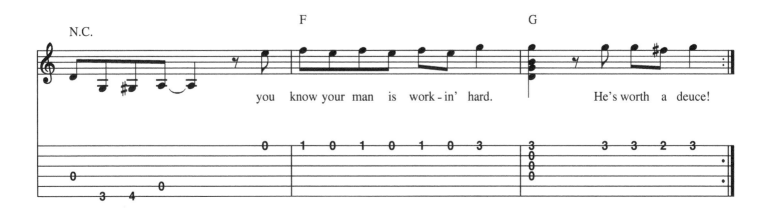

you know your man is work - in' hard. He's worth a deuce!

God of Thunder

Words and Music by Paul Stanley

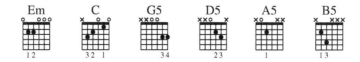

Intro
Moderate Rock
N.C. (Em)

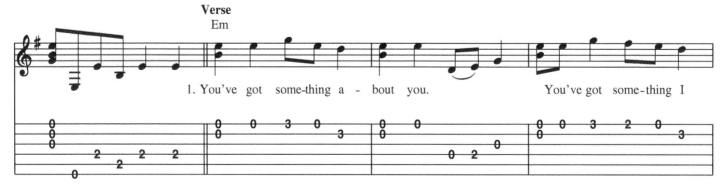

Strum Pattern: 3
Pick Pattern: 3

Verse
Em

1. You've got some-thing a - bout you. You've got some-thing I

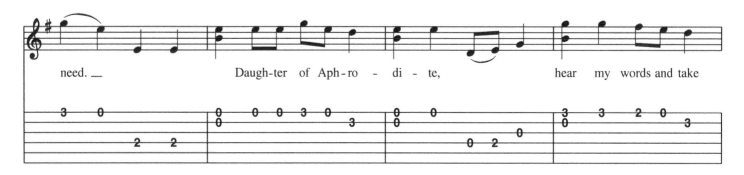

need. ___ Daugh-ter of Aph-ro - di - te, hear my words and take

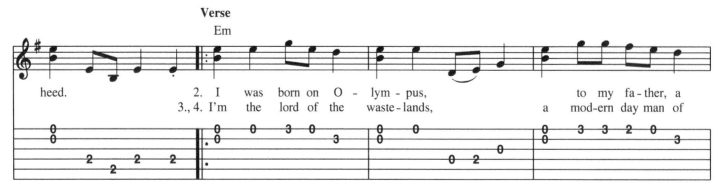

heed.
2. I was born on O - lym - pus, to my fa - ther, a
3., 4. I'm the lord of the waste - lands, a mod-ern day man of

son. ___

I was _ raised by the de - mons,   trained to reign as the

steel. ___

I gath-er dark-ness to please me,   and I com-mand you to

Chorus

one   kneel be - fore the   God of thun - der   and rock 'n' roll. ___

The spell you're un - der   will slow - ly rob you of your vir -

Outro   *play 3 times*

gin soul.

Hard Luck Woman

Words and Music by Paul Stanley

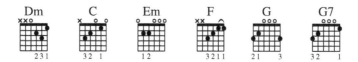

Strum Pattern: 2, 3
Pick Pattern: 2, 4

Moderately

Verse

1. If nev-er I met you, I'd nev-er have seen you cry.

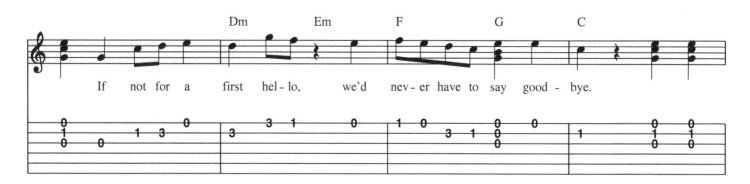

If not for a first hel-lo, we'd nev-er have to say good - bye.

Verse

2. If nev-er I held you, my feel-ings would nev-er show. It's time I start
kiss you, and wipe the tears from your eyes. I don't want to

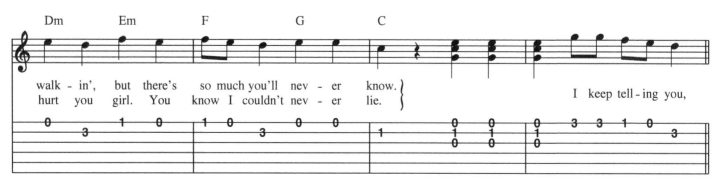

walk - in', but there's so much you'll nev - er know. I keep tell-ing you,
hurt you girl. You know I couldn't nev - er lie.

Heaven's on Fire

Words and Music by Paul Stanley and Desmond Child

Strum Pattern: 3, 4
Pick Pattern: 3, 4

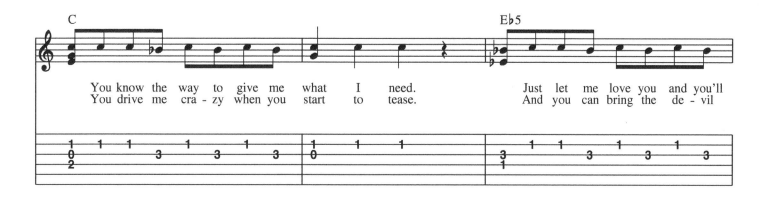

You know the way to give me what I need.
You drive me cra - zy when you start to tease. Just let me love you and you'll
And you can bring the de - vil

Chorus

ne - ver leave.
to his knees. Feel my heat tak - ing you high - er.

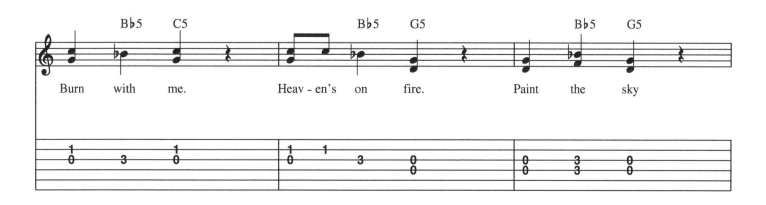

Burn with me. Heav - en's on fire. Paint the sky

D.S. al Fine
(2nd time)
Fine

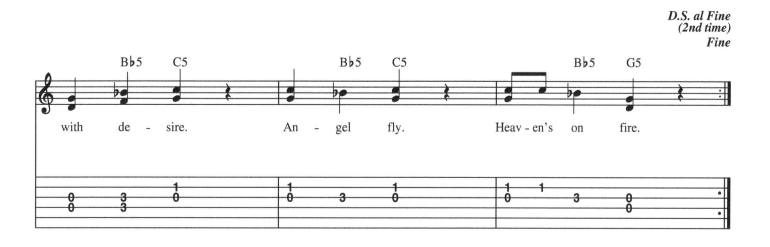

with de - sire. An - gel fly. Heav - en's on fire.

Hotter Than Hell

Words and Music by Paul Stanley

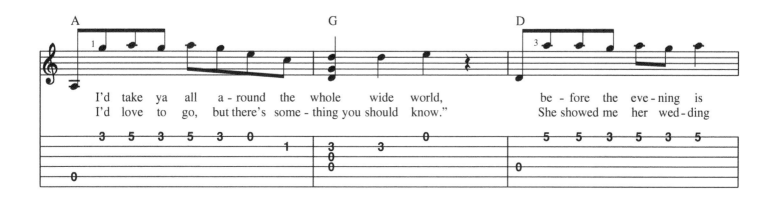

I'd take ya all a-round the whole wide world, be-fore the eve-ning is
I'd love to go, but there's some-thing you should know." She showed me her wed-ding

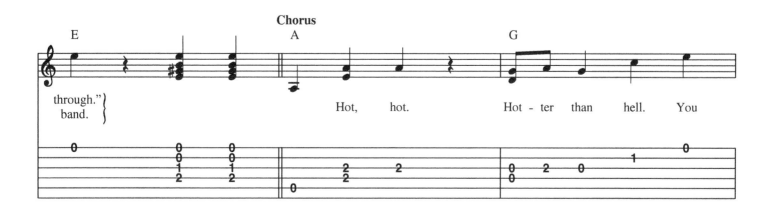

Chorus

through."
band.
Hot, hot. Hot - ter than hell. You

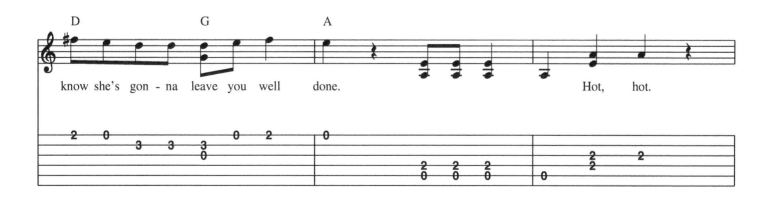

know she's gon - na leave you well done. Hot, hot.

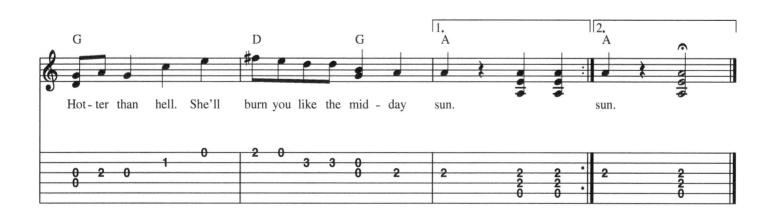

Hot - ter than hell. She'll burn you like the mid - day sun. sun.

I Was Made for Lovin' You

Words and Music by Paul Stanley, Desmond Child and Vini Poncia

Em   Am   G   B7   A

Strum Pattern: 2, 4
Pick Pattern: 2, 4

Intro
Moderately

Do, do, do, do, do, do, do, do, do. Do, do, do, do, do, do, do.

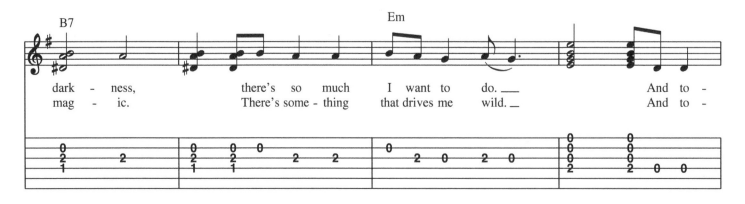

do, do, do. 1. To-night   I want to give it all to you.   In the
night   I want see to it in your eyes.   Feel the

dark-ness,   there's so much   I want to   do. ___   And to-
mag-ic.   There's some-thing   that drives me   wild. _   And to-

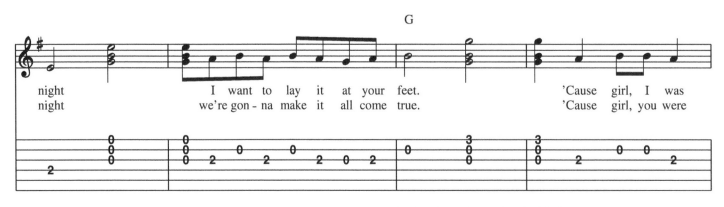

night   I want to lay it at your feet.   'Cause girl, I was
night   we're gon-na make it all come true.   'Cause girl, you were

* Sing 1st time only.

Lick It Up

Words and Music by Paul Stanley and Vincent Cusano

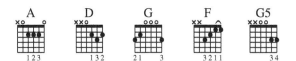

Strum Pattern: 2, 3
Pick Pattern: 2, 4

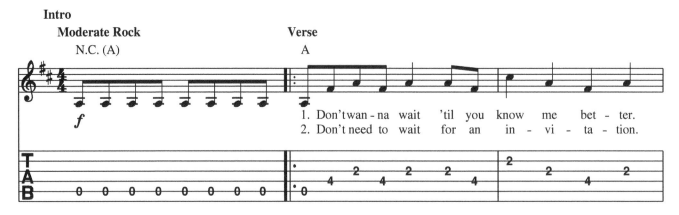

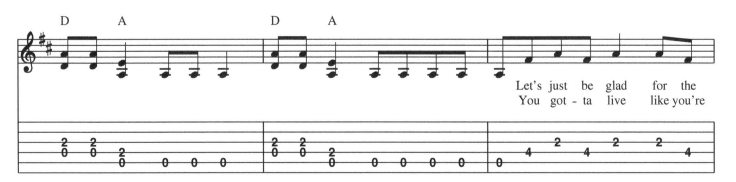

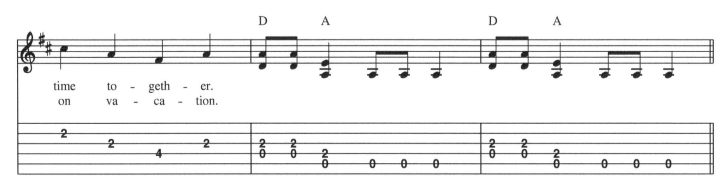

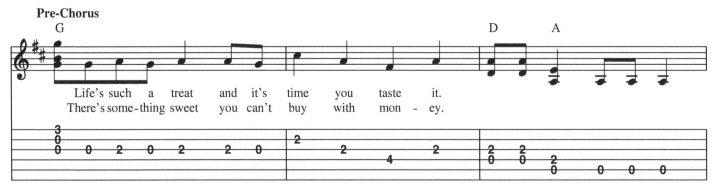

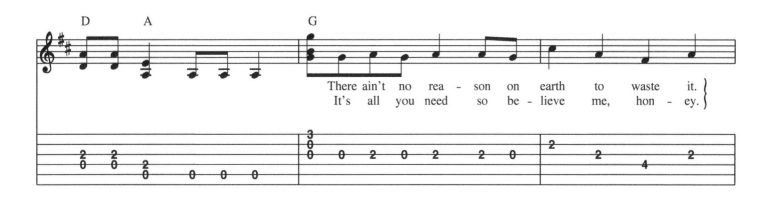

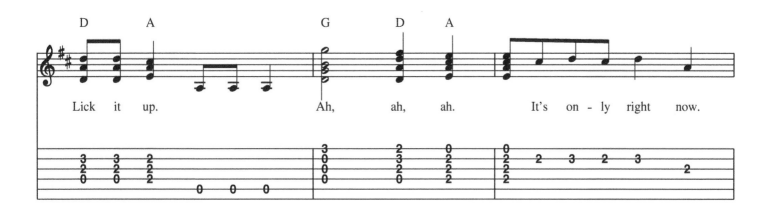

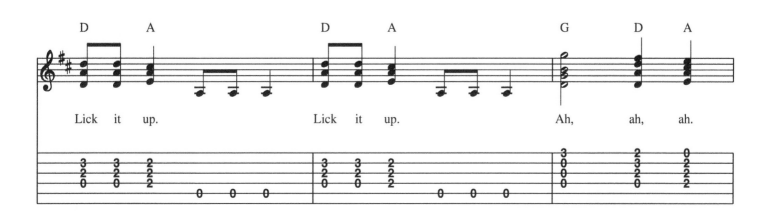

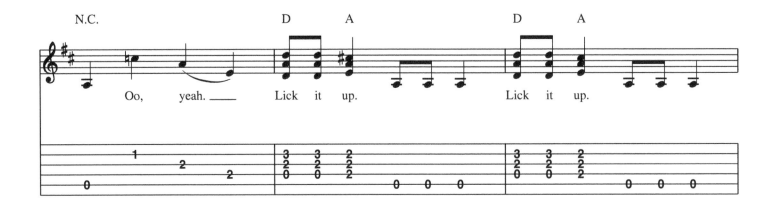

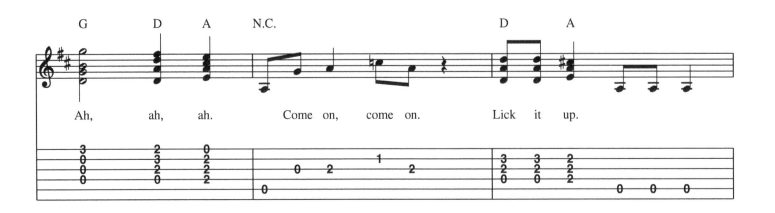

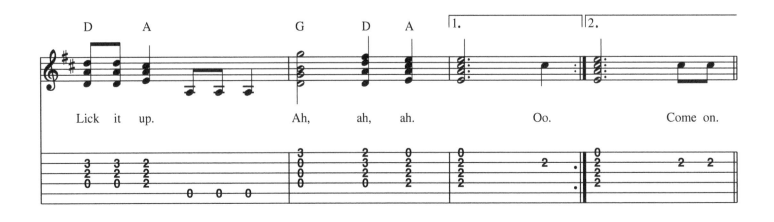

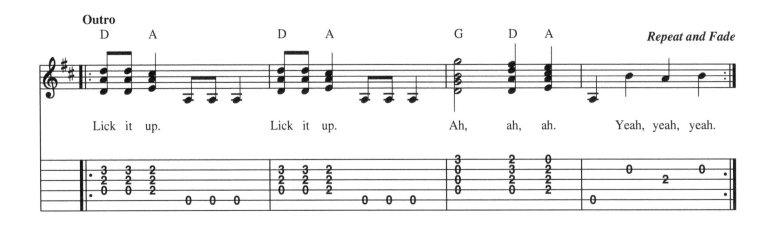

Love Gun

Words and Music by Paul Stanley

She

Words and Music by Gene Simmons and Steve Coronel

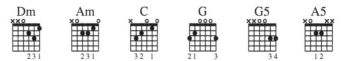

* **Strum Pattern: 8**
* **Pick Pattern: 8**

Intro
Moderately

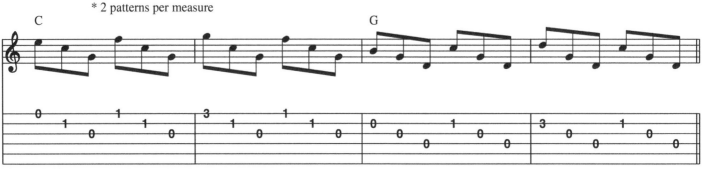

* 2 patterns per measure

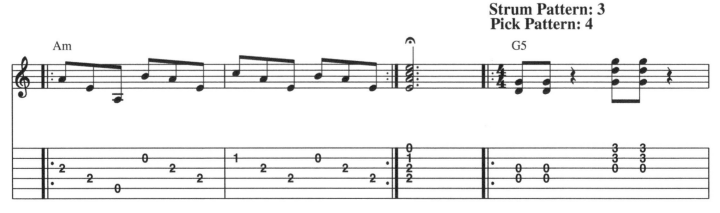

Strum Pattern: 3
Pick Pattern: 4

Verse

1. She walks by moon-light.
2. Do-ing well for oth-ers.

She

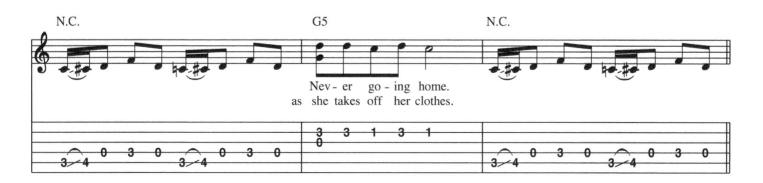

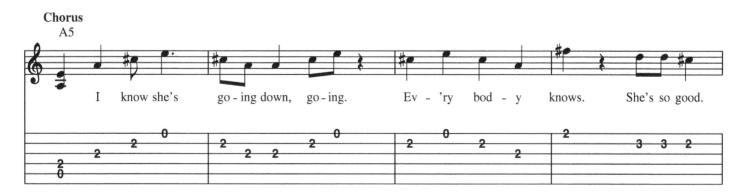

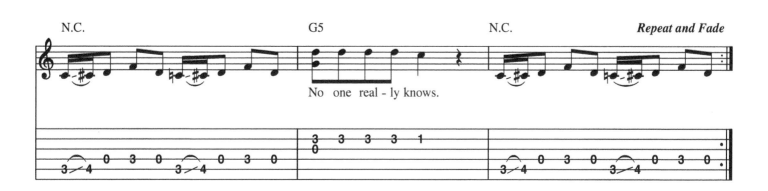

Shock Me

Words and Music by Ace Frehley

Strum Pattern: 3, 4
Pick Pattern: 3, 4

*Hold applies to chord symbols.

Shout It Out Loud

Words and Music by Paul Stanley, Gene Simmons and Bob Ezrin

Strutter

Words and Music by Paul Stanley and Gene Simmons

Strum Pattern: 1, 2
Pick Pattern: 2, 4

Intro
Moderate Rock

Verse

1., 3. I know a thing or two a -
2. She wears her sat - ins like a

bout her.
la - dy.

I know she'll on - ly make you
She gets her way just like a

cry.
child.

She'll let you walk the street be -
You take her home and she says,

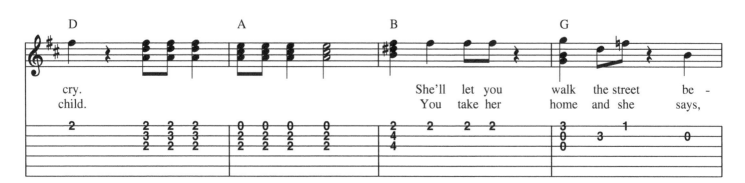

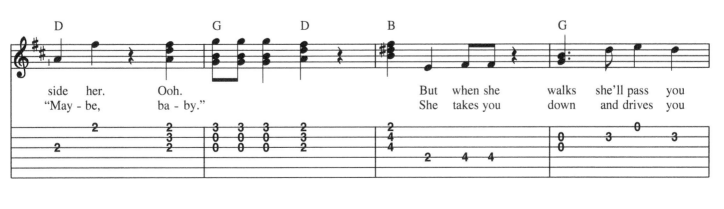

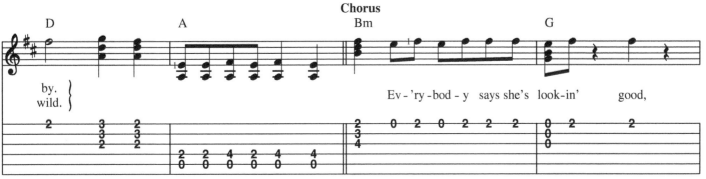

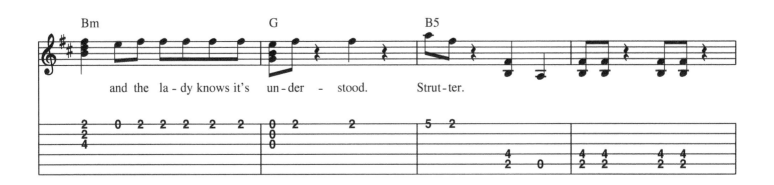

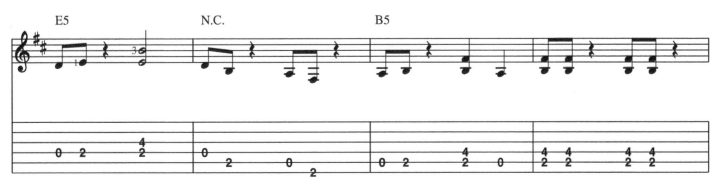

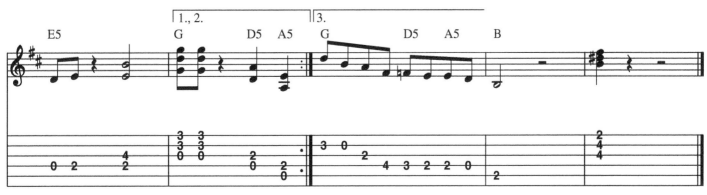

Tears Are Falling

Words and Music by Paul Stanley

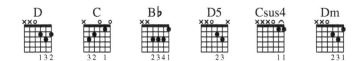

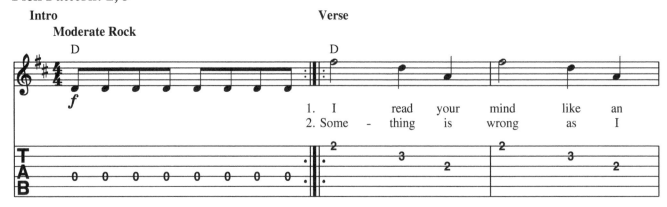

Strum Pattern: 2, 3
Pick Pattern: 2, 3

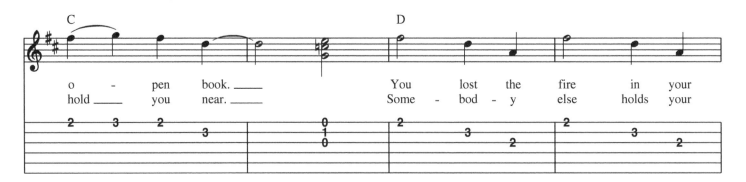

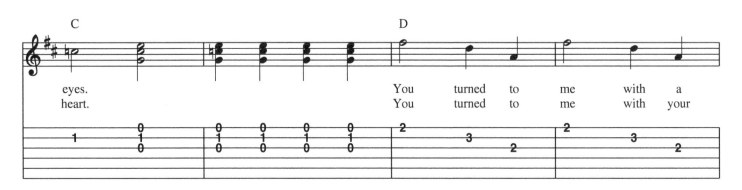

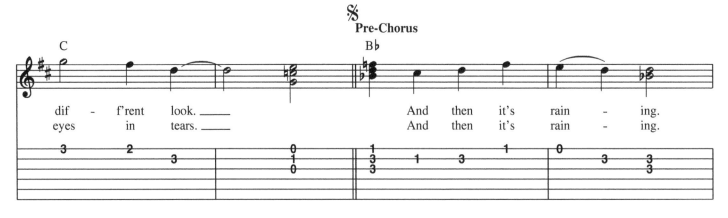

Rock and Roll All Nite

Words and Music by Paul Stanley and Gene Simmons

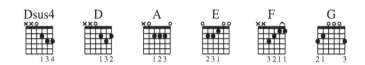

Strum Pattern: 2
Pick Pattern: 4

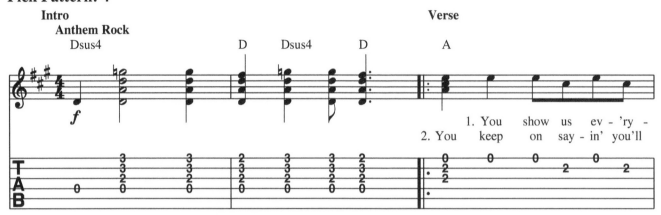

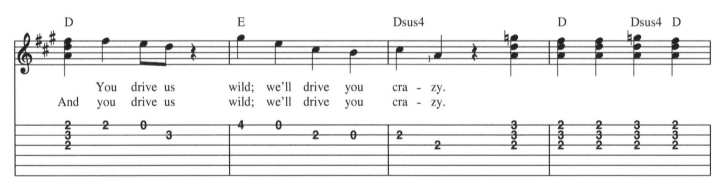

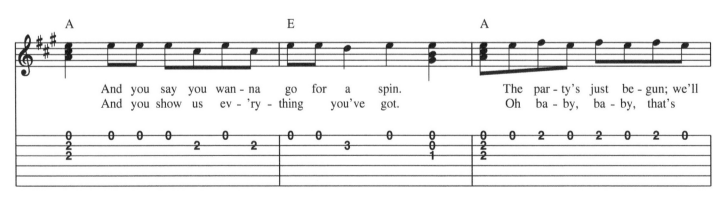

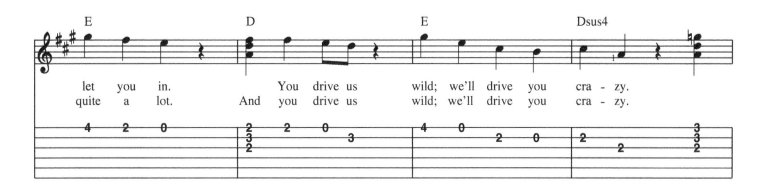

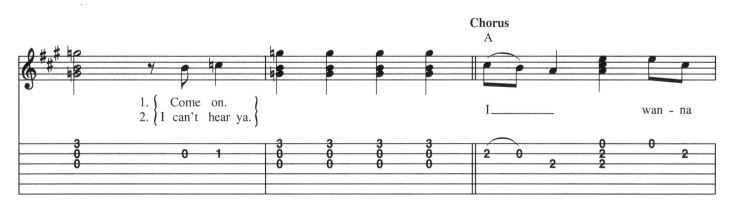

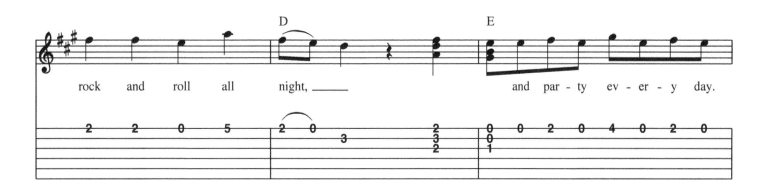

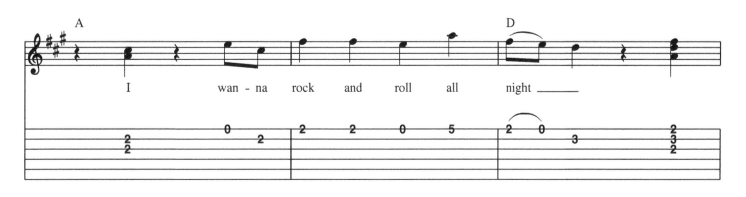

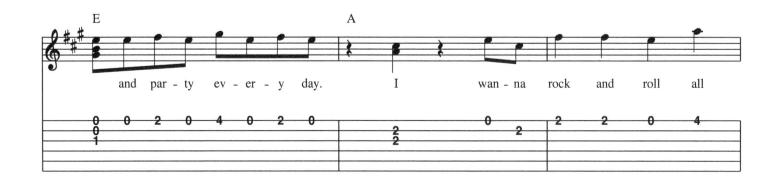

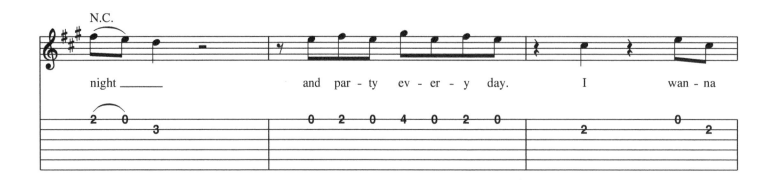

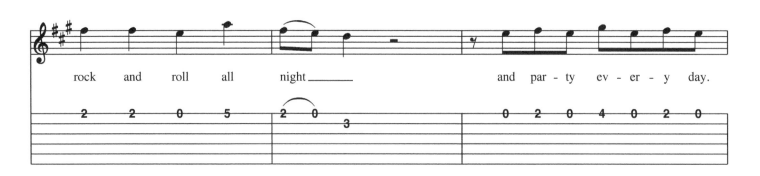

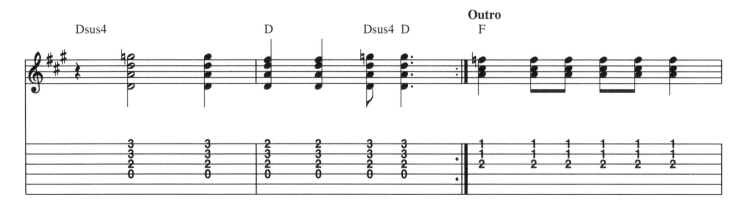

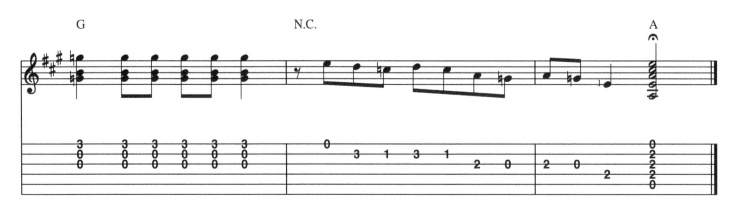

THE MOST REQUESTED SERIES

ACOUSTIC SONGS
48 songs: American Pie • Black Water • The Boxer • Cat's in the Cradle • Crazy Little Thing Called Love • Free Fallin' • Friend of the Devil • I Walk the Line • Landslide • More Than Words • Patience • Redemption Song • Summer Breeze • Toes • Wish You Were Here • and many more.

00001518 Piano/Vocal/Guitar $19.99

BOSSA NOVA & SAMBA SONGS
61 songs: Bonita • Don't Ever Go Away (Por Causa De Voce) • A Felicidade • The Girl from Ipanema (Garôta De Ipanema) • How Insensitive (Insensatez) • The Look of Love • Mas Que Nada • So Nice (Summer Samba) • Triste • and many more.

00154900 Piano/Vocal/Guitar $24.99

CHILDREN'S SONGS
73 songs: Addams Family Theme • Be Our Guest • Edelweiss • Ghostbusters • Happy Birthday to You • Linus and Lucy • Put on a Happy Face • Sing • So Long, Farewell • Take Me Out to the Ball Game • This Land Is Your Land • You Are My Sunshine • and many more.

00145525 Piano/Vocal/Guitar $19.99

CHRISTMAS SONGS
69 songs: Blue Christmas • Christmas Time Is Here • Deck the Hall • Feliz Navidad • Grandma Got Run over by a Reindeer • I'll Be Home for Christmas • Jingle Bells • Little Saint Nick • Nuttin' for Christmas • Rudolph the Red-Nosed Reindeer • Silent Night • and more.

00001563 Piano/Vocal/Guitar $24.99

CLASSIC ROCK SONGS
60 songs: Africa • Bang a Gong (Get It On) • Don't Stop Believin' • Feelin' Alright • Hello, It's Me • Layla • Life in the Fast Lane • Maybe I'm Amazed • Money • Only the Good Die Young • Small Town • Tiny Dancer • We Are the Champions • and more!

02501632 Piano/Vocal/Guitar $24.99

COUNTRY SONGS
47 songs: Cruise • Don't You Wanna Stay • Fly Over States • Gunpowder & Lead • How Do You Like Me Now?! • If I Die Young • Need You Now • Red Solo Cup • The Thunder Rolls • Wide Open Spaces • and more.

00127660 Piano/Vocal/Guitar $19.99

COUNTRY LOVE SONGS
59 songs: Always on My Mind • Amazed • Crazy • Forever and Ever, Amen • I Will Always Love You • Love Story • Stand by Your Man • Through the Years • When You Say Nothing at All • You're Still the One • and more.

00159649 Piano/Vocal/Guitar $29.99

FOLK/POP SONGS
62 songs: Blowin' in the Wind • Do You Believe in Magic • Fast Car • The House of the Rising Sun • If I Were a Carpenter • Leaving on a Jet Plane • Morning Has Broken • The Night They Drove Old Dixie Down • Puff the Magic Dragon • The Sound of Silence • Teach Your Children • and more.

00110225 Piano/Vocal/Guitar $22.99

ISLAND SONGS
60 songs: Beyond the Sea • Blue Hawaii • Coconut • Don't Worry, Be Happy • Electric Avenue • Escape (The Pina Colada Song) • I Can See Clearly Now • Island Girl • Kokomo • Redemption Song • Surfer Girl • Tiny Bubbles • and many more.

00197925 Piano/Vocal/Guitar $19.99

JAZZ STANDARDS
75 songs: All the Things You Are • Blue Skies • Embraceable You • Fascinating Rhythm • God Bless' the Child • I Got Rhythm • Mood Indigo • Pennies from Heaven • Satin Doll • Stella by Starlight • Summertime • The Very Thought of You • and more.

00102988 Piano/Vocal/Guitar $19.99

MOVIE SONGS
73 songs: Born Free • Chariots of Fire • Endless Love • I Will Always Love You • James Bond Theme • Mrs. Robinson • Moon River • Over the Rainbow • Stand by Me • Star Wars (Main Theme) • (I've Had) The Time of My Life • The Wind Beneath My Wings • and more!

00102882 Piano/Vocal/Guitar $19.99

POP/FOLK SONGS
60 songs: Alison • Annie's Song • Both Sides Now • The Boxer • California Girls • Fire and Rain • Joy to the World • Longer • Son-Of-A-Preacher Man • Summer in the City • Up on the Roof • and many more.

00145529 Piano/Vocal/Guitar $22.99

SONGS OF THE '60s
72 songs: Aquarius • The Beat Goes On • Beyond the Sea • Happy Together • Hey Jude • King of the Road • Like a Rolling Stone • Save the Last Dance for Me • Son-Of-A-Preacher Man • These Eyes • Under the Boardwalk • Up on the Roof • and more.

00110207 Piano/Vocal/Guitar $24.99

SONGS OF THE '70s
58 songs: Bohemian Rhapsody • Desperado • Hello, It's Me • I Will Survive • Just the Way You Are • Let It Be • Night Moves • Rocky Mountain High • Summer Breeze • Time in a Bottle • You're So Vain • Your Song • and many more.

00119714 Piano/Vocal/Guitar $24.99

SONGS OF THE '80s
59 songs: Africa • Billie Jean • Come on Eileen • Every Breath You Take • Faith • Footloose • Hello • Here I Go Again • Jessie's Girl • Like a Virgin • Livin' on a Prayer • Open Arms • Rosanna • Sweet Child O' Mine • Take on Me • Uptown Girl • and more.

00111668 Piano/Vocal/Guitar $27.99

SONGS OF THE '90s
51 songs: All I Wanna Do • ...Baby One More Time • Barely Breathing • Creep • Fields of Gold • From a Distance • Livin' La Vida Loca • Losing My Religion • Semi-Charmed Life • Smells like Teen Spirit • 3 AM • Under the Bridge • Who Will Save Your Soul • You Oughta Know • and more.

00111971 Piano/Vocal/Guitar $19.99

WEDDING RECEPTION SONGS
54 songs: Celebration • How Sweet It Is (To Be Loved by You) • Hungry Eyes • I Will Always Love You • In My Life • Isn't She Lovely • Last Dance • Let's Get It On • Love and Marriage • My Girl • Sunrise, Sunset • Unforgettable • The Way You Look Tonight • and more.

02501750 Piano/Vocal/Guitar $19.99

HAL•LEONARD®

EASY GUITAR WITH NOTES & TAB

This series features simplified arrangements with notes, tab, chord charts, and strum and pick patterns.

MIXED FOLIOS

00702287	Acoustic	$19.99
00702002	Acoustic Rock Hits for Easy Guitar	$17.99
00702166	All-Time Best Guitar Collection	$29.99
00702232	Best Acoustic Songs for Easy Guitar	$16.99
00119835	Best Children's Songs	$16.99
00703055	The Big Book of Nursery Rhymes & Children's Songs	$16.99
00698978	Big Christmas Collection	$19.99
00702394	Bluegrass Songs for Easy Guitar	$15.99
00289632	Bohemian Rhapsody	$19.99
00703387	Celtic Classics	$16.99
00224808	Chart Hits of 2016-2017	$14.99
00267383	Chart Hits of 2017-2018	$14.99
00334293	Chart Hits of 2019-2020	$16.99
00403479	Chart Hits of 2021-2022	$16.99
00702149	Children's Christian Songbook	$9.99
00702028	Christmas Classics	$9.99
00101779	Christmas Guitar	$16.99
00702141	Classic Rock	$8.95
00159642	Classical Melodies	$12.99
00253933	Disney/Pixar's Coco	$19.99
00702203	CMT's 100 Greatest Country Songs	$34.99
00702283	The Contemporary Christian Collection	$16.99

00196954	Contemporary Disney	$19.99
00702239	Country Classics for Easy Guitar	$24.99
00702257	Easy Acoustic Guitar Songs	$17.99
00702041	Favorite Hymns for Easy Guitar	$12.99
00222701	Folk Pop Songs	$19.99
00126894	Frozen	$14.99
00333922	Frozen 2	$14.99
00702286	Glee	$16.99
00702160	The Great American Country Songbook	$19.99
00702148	Great American Gospel for Guitar	$14.99
00702050	Great Classical Themes for Easy Guitar	$9.99
00148030	Halloween Guitar Songs	$17.99
00702273	Irish Songs	$14.99
00192503	Jazz Classics for Easy Guitar	$16.99
00702275	Jazz Favorites for Easy Guitar	$17.99
00702274	Jazz Standards for Easy Guitar	$19.99
00702162	Jumbo Easy Guitar Songbook	$24.99
00232285	La La Land	$16.99
00702258	Legends of Rock	$14.99
00702189	MTV's 100 Greatest Pop Songs	$34.99
00702272	1950s Rock	$16.99
00702271	1960s Rock	$16.99
00702270	1970s Rock	$24.99
00702269	1980s Rock	$16.99

00702268	1990s Rock	$24.99
00369043	Rock Songs for Kids	$14.99
00109725	Once	$14.99
00702187	Selections from O Brother Where Art Thou?	$19.99
00702178	100 Songs for Kids	$16.99
00702515	Pirates of the Caribbean	$17.99
00702125	Praise and Worship for Guitar	$14.99
00287930	Songs from *A Star Is Born, The Greatest Showman, La La Land,* and More Movie Musicals	$16.99
00702285	Southern Rock Hits	$12.99
00156420	Star Wars Music	$16.99
00121535	30 Easy Celtic Guitar Solos	$16.99
00244654	Top Hits of 2017	$14.99
00283786	Top Hits of 2018	$14.99
00302269	Top Hits of 2019	$14.99
00355779	Top Hits of 2020	$14.99
00374083	Top Hits of 2021	$16.99
00702294	Top Worship Hits	$17.99
00702255	VH1's 100 Greatest Hard Rock Songs	$39.99
00702175	VH1's 100 Greatest Songs of Rock and Roll	$34.99
00702253	Wicked	$12.99

ARTIST COLLECTIONS

00702267	AC/DC for Easy Guitar	$17.99
00156221	Adele – 25	$16.99
00396889	Adele – 30	$19.99
00702040	Best of the Allman Brothers	$16.99
00702865	J.S. Bach for Easy Guitar	$15.99
00702169	Best of The Beach Boys	$16.99
00702292	The Beatles — 1	$22.99
00125796	Best of Chuck Berry	$16.99
00702201	The Essential Black Sabbath	$15.99
00702250	blink-182 — Greatest Hits	$19.99
02501615	Zac Brown Band — The Foundation	$19.99
02501621	Zac Brown Band — You Get What You Give	$16.99
00702043	Best of Johnny Cash	$19.99
00702090	Eric Clapton's Best	$16.99
00702086	Eric Clapton — from the Album Unplugged	$17.99
00702202	The Essential Eric Clapton	$19.99
00702053	Best of Patsy Cline	$17.99
00222697	Very Best of Coldplay – 2nd Edition	$17.99
00702229	The Very Best of Creedence Clearwater Revival	$16.99
00702145	Best of Jim Croce	$16.99
00702278	Crosby, Stills & Nash	$12.99
14042809	Bob Dylan	$15.99
00702276	Fleetwood Mac — Easy Guitar Collection	$17.99
00139462	The Very Best of Grateful Dead	$17.99
00702136	Best of Merle Haggard	$19.99
00702227	Jimi Hendrix — Smash Hits	$19.99
00702288	Best of Hillsong United	$12.99
00702236	Best of Antonio Carlos Jobim	$15.99

00702245	Elton John — Greatest Hits 1970–2002	$19.99
00129855	Jack Johnson	$17.99
00702204	Robert Johnson	$16.99
00702234	Selections from Toby Keith — 35 Biggest Hits	$12.95
00702003	Kiss	$16.99
00702216	Lynyrd Skynyrd	$17.99
00702182	The Essential Bob Marley	$17.99
00146081	Maroon 5	$14.99
00121925	Bruno Mars – Unorthodox Jukebox	$12.99
00702248	Paul McCartney — All the Best	$14.99
00125484	The Best of MercyMe	$12.99
00702209	Steve Miller Band — Young Hearts (Greatest Hits)	$12.95
00124167	Jason Mraz	$15.99
00702096	Best of Nirvana	$17.99
00702211	The Offspring — Greatest Hits	$17.99
00138026	One Direction	$17.99
00702030	Best of Roy Orbison	$17.99
00702144	Best of Ozzy Osbourne	$14.99
00702279	Tom Petty	$17.99
00102911	Pink Floyd	$17.99
00702139	Elvis Country Favorites	$19.99
00702293	The Very Best of Prince	$22.99
00699415	Best of Queen for Guitar	$16.99
00109279	Best of R.E.M.	$14.99
00702208	Red Hot Chili Peppers — Greatest Hits	$19.99
00198960	The Rolling Stones	$17.99
00174793	The Very Best of Santana	$16.99
00702196	Best of Bob Seger	$16.99
00146046	Ed Sheeran	$19.99

00702252	Frank Sinatra — Nothing But the Best	$12.99
00702010	Best of Rod Stewart	$17.99
00702049	Best of George Strait	$17.99
00702259	Taylor Swift for Easy Guitar	$15.99
00359800	Taylor Swift – Easy Guitar Anthology	$24.99
00702260	Taylor Swift — Fearless	$14.99
00139727	Taylor Swift — 1989	$19.99
00115960	Taylor Swift — Red	$16.99
00253667	Taylor Swift — Reputation	$17.99
00702290	Taylor Swift — Speak Now	$16.99
00232849	Chris Tomlin Collection – 2nd Edition	$14.99
00702226	Chris Tomlin — See the Morning	$12.95
00148643	Train	$14.99
00702427	U2 — 18 Singles	$19.99
00702108	Best of Stevie Ray Vaughan	$17.99
00279005	The Who	$14.99
00702123	Best of Hank Williams	$15.99
00194548	Best of John Williams	$14.99
00702228	Neil Young — Greatest Hits	$17.99
00119133	Neil Young — Harvest	$16.99

Prices, contents and availability subject to change without notice.

Visit Hal Leonard online at halleonard.com